Using thi

When going through this book
with your child, you can either read through
the story first, talking about it
and discussing the pictures,
or start with the sounds pages
at the beginning.

If you start at the front of the book,
read the words and point to the pictures.
Emphasise the **sound** of the letter.

Encourage your child to think
of the other words beginning with
and including the same sound.
The story gives you the opportunity
to point out these sounds.

After the story, slowly go through the
sounds pages at the end.

Always praise and encourage
as you go along. Keep your
reading sessions short and stop
if your child loses interest.

Throughout the series, the order in which the sounds
are introduced has been carefully planned to
help the important link between reading and writing.
This link has proved to be a powerful boost to
the development of both skills.

SOUNDS FEATURED IN THIS BOOK
b p k bl br pr
pl ph kn

The sounds introduced are repeated
and given emphasis in the practice books,
where the link between reading and writing is at the
root of the activities and games.

Ladybird books are widely available, but in case of
difficulty may be ordered by post or telephone from:

Ladybird Books – Cash Sales Department
Littlegate Road Paignton Devon TQ3 3BE
Telephone 0803 554761

A catalogue record for this book is available
from the British Library

Published by Ladybird Books Ltd Loughborough Leicestershire UK
Ladybird Books Inc Auburn Maine 04210 USA

Text copyright © Jill Corby 1993
© LADYBIRD BOOKS LTD 1993

Say the Sounds
Pirate's treasure

by JILL CORBY
illustrated by RAY MUTIMER

Bb

Say the sound.

bag

bell

be

beach

biscuit

bed

book

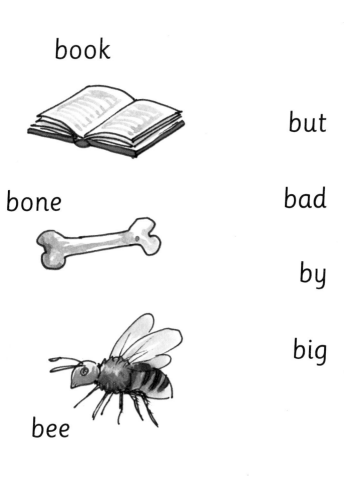

but

bone

bad

by

big

bee

Pp

parrot

pipe

pool

pirate

 pink

pit

put

poppy

port

pip

lap

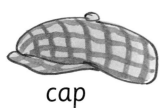

cap

tap

lip

Kk

Say the sound.

kettle

kangaroo

king

kitten

end

tank

sink

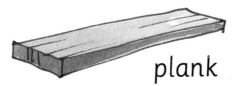

plank

thank

pink

Kevin is on his big bulldozer.
He sees Ben and Jenny.
They are going down to the
beach.

Ben sees Kevin and his
big bulldozer.

They like it on the sand on the beach.

They like to jump on the sand.

"Look, Ben, look. I can see a ship," says Jenny.

"Yes, I can see a ship, too," says Ben. "It is a pirate ship."

"Look, here comes the
pirate now," Jenny tells Ben.

"He's coming to the beach.
He's coming very quickly,"
Ben says.

"Yes, he's coming very quickly," Jenny tells Ben. "And he's very big."

They can see the big pirate
coming over the sand now.

"Come in here quickly, Ben,"
Jenny says. "Down, Ben,
down."

The big pirate is looking
down at the beach. He is
looking everywhere.

"What can he be looking for?" asks Jenny.

"Look at the pirate now," Jenny tells Ben. "Look at him."

"He is looking everywhere," Ben says to Jenny.

"I can't find it," the pirate says. He is so sad.

"It is not here," the pirate tells them.
"What is not here?" asks Jenny.

"What are you looking for?" asks Ben.
"The map," the pirate tells them. "The map is not here."

"I must find the map and I must find the treasure," he tells them.

"Are you looking for treasure here?" asks Ben.
"Yes. There is a map and there is treasure on this beach," the pirate tells Ben.

"Then we are going to help you to find your map," Jenny says.
"We must help you to look everywhere for your map," says Ben.

The pirate lets them look for his map. Then Ben finds the map.

"Is this your map?" he asks.
"Yes. This is the map," the
pirate tells Ben and Jenny.

Ben and Jenny help the pirate.
They can see a tree, a pool
and a big stone on the map.
They look for a tree, a pool
and a big stone.

"I can see them!" shouts Ben.
"Look at them over there,"
he says.

"The map says seven steps from this pool and seven steps from this tree and seven steps from this big stone," the pirate says.

"Let's step it out now and see. Let's step it out from here."

"I think it will be here,"
Jenny tells them.
"And I think it will be here,"
Ben says.

"Let's step it out and see,"
the pirate tells them.
"I think it will be here."

The sand is too hard. The pirate can't dig the hard sand.

Jenny has an idea. It is a good idea. She shouts out to Kevin on the bulldozer. "Please will you come over here on your bulldozer, Kevin?"

"That is a good idea, Jenny," the pirate says.

The pirate says, "Dig here please, Kevin."
The bulldozer digs the hard sand. It finds the treasure in the hard sand.

The pirate is so pleased that he has the treasure.

He is so pleased that he lets Jenny and Ben have a present. He lets Kevin have a present, too.

Ben, Jenny and Kevin are pleased with the presents.

bl

Say the sounds.

bleed

blue

black

block

br

brick

bridge

branch

brush   brown

pr

Say the sounds.

princess

pray

promise

present

pl

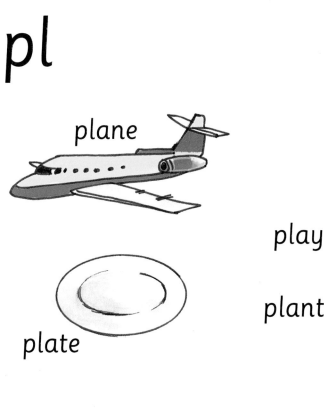

plane

plate

play

plant

plum

Say the sounds.

end **p**

cup

help

sip

tip

top

map

ph
sounds like f

elephant

dolphin

alphabet

telephone

photograph

41

kn sounds like n

knight

know

kneel

knee

New words used in the story

Words introduced 41

Learn to read with Ladybird

Read with me

A scheme of 16 graded books which uses a look-say approach to introduce beginner readers to the first 300 most frequently used words in the English language (Key Words). Children learn whole words and, with practice and repetition, build up a reading vocabulary.

Support material: Pre-reader, Practice and Play Books, Book and Cassette Packs, Picture Dictionary, Picture Word Cards

Say the Sounds

A phonically based, graded reading scheme of 8 titles. It teaches children the sounds of individual letters and letter combinations, enabling them to feel confident in approaching Key Words.

Support material:
Practice Books, Double Cassette Pack, Flash Cards

Read it yourself

A graded series of 24 books to help children to learn new words in the context of a familiar story. These readers follow on from the pre-reading series, **Read together**, and can be used in conjunction with any Ladybird reading scheme.